The Gulf Coast of FLORIDA

The Gulf Coast of FLORIDA

Photography by
Richard Riley

Introduction by
John D. MacDonald

Produced by Roger Boulton Publishing Services, Toronto
Designed by Fortunato Aglialoro

©1984 Oxford University Press (Canadian Branch)
SKYLINE PRESS is a registered imprint of the Oxford University Press

ISBN 0-19-540621-4
1 2 3 4 – 7 6 5 4
Printed in Hong Kong by Scanner Art Services, Inc., Toronto

Introduction

Richard Riley has been capturing in time and space his special images of the vanishing Florida scene. I have been trying to do the same thing with words for many years. The eye of the writer and the eye of the photographer see similar shadows and fantasies.

Technical perfection is not enough. Postcards are wonders of perfection. There must be an emotional additive, a flavor imparted by the knowledge of where each particular image fits in time and space. The image must be intellectualized to have weight and meaning. Here we deal with vanishing things. The flavor is called wistful. Look at it now—a good long loving look at the pelican squadron, the ceremonies of fiddler crabs, the magic sand-writing done by the beach grasses in the sea wind, the rose dazzle and mist of first morning. And we can look with less love at the brute intrusion of structure and human use into places which Hernando DeSoto reported as being forever unfit for human habitation.

There will always be wild places in Florida. But as this century winds down they have become ever smaller and more rare. Even though most of these photographs were taken very recently, many of them could never be taken again in the same place of the same scenes, the same life forms. Many are changed and some are gone. And this is what we try to do with the pictures and the words—lock onto something vanishing—in wistfulness and wonder.

We do the west coast of Florida, not just because we know it better but because it seems at once wilder and gentler. Over there on the Atlantic side it is a simpler pattern, where an ocean hammers a coast into long flat lines. Here we have the swamps and the bayous, the winding creeks and at times such a stillness of sea and sky it is difficult to remember when the great roaring, shrieking engines of wind came careening up the Gulf, drowning and smashing.

Start up there at Pensacola, elevation 13 feet. In Escambia County, and no one remembers where the name Escambia came from. Offshore is Santa Rosa Island, twenty-five miles long. The western seven miles of it is Fort Pickens State Park. A good place to browse and look, the Gulf on one side of you, Florida Bay on the other. The Intracoastal Waterway goes inside the barrier island. Boat people with shallow draft craft move in close, pick spots of relative wilderness to come ashore.

The next county east is Santa Rosa, where the treat for the eyes and spirit is the Blackwater River, happily anchored by the Blackwater River State Park and the Blackwater River State Forest. The river winds through hilly wooded country. It is dark with tannin and looks even darker because of the whiteness of the sandbars around almost every curve in the river. An easy two day canoe trip in a good season (April or October) is worth every minute of it. High bluffs above you with hardwoods and pines, while down below a canopy of cypress, cedars and red maple. Portages few and short.

The highway past Fort Walton beach cuts through high sand dunes. In past years in February and March the fragrant white bloom of the ironwood tree along with the pastels of the flowering lupine and the plumes of the Mexican firebush made this sandy passage a thing of beauty. But the area has been 'improved' and the natural flowering is rare and sparse.

Over in Walton County, if you can get hold of a shallow draft skiff in Choctawhatchee Bay, you can poke around north of the Point Washington Wildlife Management Area into some little watery pockets with great names: Buck Bayou, Mack Bayou, Hogtown Bayou, Mussett Bayou, Jolly Bay, Bunker Cove. Some are forgettable because they've been built up. The wild ones you remember, no matter how ravenous the salt marsh bugs might be. A bird on the wing, tilting in the right light over the right waterway, is magic indeed.

Move east to Panama City in Bay County, which may have the most miles of shore line of any county in the state. St Andrew's State Park grabbed prime beach land at the entrance to St Andrew's Bay—a thousand acres of beaches and dunes on the Gulf saved forever, one hopes, from the concrete disasters happening just west of the park.

St Joseph's State Park next door in Gulf County should be more of the same, but it is quite different in a way hard to describe. Walk some of the Gulf Beach that extends ten miles north and ten miles south of Eagle Bay. Oh yes we have the parks, the bits of wildness, but so pitifully few considering the size and diversity of our subtropical peninsula. And a park overused—too many feet tramping it, too much litter, too much electronic noise—and it becomes something else. A playpen perhaps. When a thousand people use an area and two percent are natural slobs, it is reasonably unspoiled. When ten thousand use it, there are two hundred slobs and they leave their spoor.

The Apalachicola National Forest is too huge for any kind of tourist use to despoil—I think. At least so far. It spreads across more than half of Wakulla County on Apalachee Bay, and a good half of Liberty County inland. It contains a Wildlife Management Area and a Wildlife Refuge. The Ochlockonee River cuts right down through the middle of the forest preserve, and it makes for fine canoeing. The enemy of the forest is its own size. The harvesting of timber and pulpwood has become big business in its half million acres, with over twenty-five million board feet of logs trucked out each year. Also too many mining interests are smacking their lips, saying to their elected representatives—'Hell, it's so dang big, a couple drill rigs in there isn't going to hurt none, now is they?'

So we prowl on down around the perimeter of the armpit where panhandle turns slowly to peninsula, through Taylor, Dixie, Levy and Citrus counties, all fronting—or backing—on the Gulf, taking the little roads, looking for things the way they used to be, and will not be for very much longer. Wistful places and quiet times. Great swamps, seabird refuges, a glimpse of a deer, a bobcat, or one of the recent arrivals, an armadillo.

One of the great canoe trails runs almost all the way around Citrus County, in the Withlacoochee River. We are into the area of big springs that well up through the limestone with such force they make mounds of clear water on the surface of the river. The city of St Petersburg bought one, capped it, and piped the flow all the way down to the city thus predicting the probable future of the rest of them. But for now they are tourist attractions. Some with mermaids.

Then we have the feeling of emerging from an earlier world as we approach Tarpon Springs. We have come from the swamps and silences into the frenetic coast. Clearwater, St Pete, Tampa Bay, Bradenton, Sarasota, Venice, Punta Gorda, Fort Myers, Naples—each one creeping north and south along the coast to merge with neighbor cities to form a tourist strip of time shares, condos, hot concrete, fast food, sun lotion, frisbees, boom boxes, shopping malls and endless acres of parked cars glinting and shimmering in the sunshine. Here the wildness no longer comes down to the edge of the sea. You have to go inland to find peace and beauty, to Myakka Park, or far up the river at Fort Myers, or inland from Naples then south to Everglades City. Now there is a causeway across Chokoluskee Bay to Chokoluskee Island, but even before the causeway was built there was a substantial little community built entirely on a gigantic mound of shells discarded by the Calusa Indians who must have been the most avid seafood addicts in all history. It took hundreds of thousands of tons of empty shell to form that high island of many acres.

One of the places which is a distillation of that sense of disappearing wonder which this book is styled to impart is Corkscrew Swamp in the northern part of Collier County, where Audubon has a board walk which curves through an ancient swamp that grew over thousands of years on the Tamiami Formation of the Miocene, on creamy white limestone, greenish gray marls, silty sands and clay. Hope for a glimpse of a Wood Stork or an Everglades Kite, as neither will share this planet with us much longer.

An appropriate suggestion for a further experience of the feeling of timelessness, which we can suspect must be a false impression, would be to get a shallow draft skiff and a guide who knows the 'Glades, and poke around the ten thousand islands...Faka Union Bay, Pumpkin Bay, Fakahatchee Bay, down to the mouth of the Shark River where in the early spring the more enterprising fishermen go after baby tarpon with bass plugs and plug casting rods, releasing them as fast as they catch them. That silvery and inedible fish, in its infancy, when hooked will spend more time in the air than in the water. From the bones we find, we know the Indians ate them, but modern science has yet to discover a way to make tarpon meat edible, or even chewable.

In among the mangrove islands, upstream from Gullivan Bay, up past Coon Key, Panther Key, Hog Key, Mound Key, up past the interior bays and into the runoff rivers, Whitney, Wood, East, Fakahatchee, you are into the ultimate wetlands. These are fragile lands. We have seen smaller wetlands, estuaries, swamps and bogs as we worked our way down the coast. Life in these patches, and in the 'Glades, is fragile because it is interdependent to a degree not seen in the uplands. The problem of existence has caused more specialization. Wipe out a rare variety of tree snail and the Everglades Kite becomes extinct.

It does not help much to learn that seven thousand acres of wetlands disappear each year in Florida as areas are 'developed'. How can this be? Wetlands are the recharge areas for our water supply, and estuaries and grass flats are the nursery areas for the marine life which used to support a healthier commercial and sports fishing industry. Florida is loaded with ardent conservationists who see what is happening and deplore it. Yet it goes on. Why?

The answer is simple and saddening. Most of the people elected to public office on the state and county level make their living from growth and construction and development. They are lawyers, real estate dealers, brokers, ranchers, builders. In office they control the legislation. Time and time again laws are proposed which would deal fairly and firmly with conservation, but with rare exceptions these laws are gutted before they reach the Governor's desk. Though a minority of the office-holders are sincere and knowledgeable and apprehensive about our future, the majority are self-serving, indifferent, ignorant and disdainful of the 'ecofreaks'. Thus we hope this book can serve some small useful purpose in showing a world that was, a world that in many parts still is, and a world that can be preserved for the future.

So now we are off again, down the long strange chain of the Florida Keys to Key West. These keys were built up from the sea bed by untold trillions of tiny sea critters. The keys are segments of a great dead coral reef, unlike the barrier islands along the west coast. Those islands were created when Florida was lifting itself out of the sea, and great rivers carried the limestone remains of aeons of sea life out into the Gulf to form alluvial islands. Transient sand and mud has accreted to the ends and the shores of these islands, but the heart of them is tough, solid, compacted limestone.

The John Pennekamp Coral Reef State Park is one hundred square miles of underwater wonderment, with living coral to demonstrate what built the long chain of keys from Largo to Key West.

And at the end of it all, at the opposite end of the journey from Pensacola down the coast is a place where it is a local custom for people to gather together and watch the sunset, and applaud it.

I can think of no other place where scenery is applauded.

JOHN D. MACDONALD

(right) Sea oats and sand dunes, Longboat Key

Sailing south to Passagrille Beach

(right) Gulf of Mexico from Boca Grande shoreline

(left) Aerial view of intercoastal waters, Destin

Pelican, Key West

Downtown detail, Key West

(right) Double-masted schooner at anchor in Sarasota's intercoastal waters

Sailing under cumulus clouds, intercoastal waters, Sarasota

(right) Sailing in Tampa Bay at midday, out from St Pete harbor

Art show, Cedar Key

(right) Window display, Key West

(left) Clothing boutiques, Key West

Fort Walton Beach

Sailing north of Dunedin

(right) Lilypads cover a pond in the Everglades

(left) Net fishing off Mexico Beach

Mullet fishing with shore-net, late afternoon, Mexico Beach

US 1 looking east, Florida Keys

Mangroves, Florida Keys

(left) Downtown, Key West

Sailing west towards St Petersburg pier

(left) Sunning on Laguna's beach

Old track to Boca Grande

(left) Sarasota, '40s style
Fire-station porch, Cedar Key

Sailing along Clearwater Beach

(right) Wind-rippled sand dunes, Destin

Fishing boats, East Point

(right) Fishing boats under construction, Tarpon Springs

(left) Sunset on Highway 98

Steam locomotive on display, Pensacola

(left) Oyster boats at sunrise, East Point Causeway, Clearwater Beach

Coal barge for the power-plant,
Fort Myers

(right) Masts at sunset, Clearwater Marina

(left) Skeletal tree, Longboat Key

Gulf of Mexico, Longboat Key

(left) Birdseye view of a sandbar, Destin

Windblown white heron, Clearwater Beach

Garden decoration, Crystal River
(right) Classical mansion, Crystal River

Late afternoon, Key West

Rainstorm, Lighthouse Point

Cottage yard, Key West

(right) Banyans, Boca Grande

(left) Sunset light, Palm Harbor

Sidewalk tranquillity, Palm Harbor

Seven-mile bridge, Florida Keys
(right) Fishing nets, Cedar Key

(left) Seagulls on a pier in morning light, Cedar Key

Golden tones, Destin

Sailboat race, Sarasota Bay

(right) Fishing boat, Apalachicola

Old locomotive, Pensacola
(right) Tavern at sunset, Pensacola

(left) Bottom-fishing, Pensacola

Gazebo at sunset, Pensacola

(left) Clearwater Causeway

Marco Island at sunset

Spinnaker running downwind, Palm Harbor

Fort Jefferson, Dry Tortugas

Key West

Country store, Cedar Key

(left) Treeline at sunset, Palm Harbor

St Petersburg Beach

(left) Traps waiting for the season, Florida Keys

Vinoy Yacht Basin, St Pete

Thunderclouds on the western horizon, Florida Keys

(right) Rainshowers in late afternoon, Florida Keys

Boats in harbor, Tarpon Springs

(right) Fountain at the entrance to Ringling Brothers Museum, Sarasota

(left) St Petersburg pier

Dunedin Causeway

Morning light, Cedar Key

(right) Cedar Key skyline

Harbor, Port St Joe

(right) Boatyard construction, Port St Joe

Looking north in Yankee Town

(right) Looking west across grassy knolls from Everglades City

(left) Clearwater Beach

Cedar Key sunrise

St Petersburg skyline at sunrise

Lightning storm over downtown Clearwater

Fourth of July, Clearwater Beach

Evening sail, Naples

(left) Old fish-house at sunrise, mackerel skies

US 1 looking south

Sailing in the Gulf of Mexico off Madena Beach